Drown the Shadow

Lauren Sherman

Presentation by *BookLeaf Publishing*

Web: www.bookleafpub.com

E-mail: info@bookleafpub.com

ISBN: 9789357212830

First edition 2023

For April. To show you that beyond your comfort zone lies a world of possibilities. xXx

Unhurried Expansion

Entrenched roots descending deeper
A firm grip; taking hold
Spreading, reaching, yearning, seeking
Searching for my truth untold

Stronger roots. Stable foundations.
Unswerving in the strongest wind
The more I search the more I find
The stronger that my roots set in.

There is no rush in this adventure
Endless as the rolling skies
A journey inwards ever onwards
Continuously I grow. I rise.

Projection

It's a truth that it's uncomfortable
To confront what lies within
That there's a monster that's in each of us
That leads us all to sin

It's easy to turn outwards
And not confront ourselves
To avoid the pain of who we are
By blaming someone else

But projection will not help us
It will not help us gain
Short term relief does nothing more than yield
more long term pain

For projection does not shine a light or unify us
all
It just transfers the suffering
And causes us to fall

Instead surrender fully to the monster that's your
own,
Accept that it's your monster and that it's yours
and yours alone.

The Puzzle Piece

I'm told theres something missing
That something doesn't fit
I'm told that there is something wrong
That's with my brain that is.

You see i'm not your average person
I'm "blunt, rude and direct"
But it's not intentional
I mean no disrespect

I can't control emotions
Or deal with sudden sounds
I cannot cope with textures
Or with smells or tastes I've found

I thrive on continuity and a sense of a routine
If something goes off kilter I get overwhelmed
you see

I don't know how to function when I am
overwhelmed
I withdraw, shut down or panic
I go into my shell

Eye contact can be painful,
And certain touch can hurt.
Just the right amount of pressure
For this awkward introvert

I have my special interests
That absorb my mind for days
Each time I find a new one
I'm told it's just "another phase"

I'm literal and honest
And I have had to learn
To navigate a minefield
Of words, phrases and turns

I'm told that I'm a puzzle piece and that I really
should fit in,
That I need to learn to function in this world I'm
living in

But i'm not a missing puzzle piece
or a riddle to be solved
There's nothing that needs fixing
I just don't fit the mold

For I have alot to offer
With my brain that's different
I'm loving kind and caring
Bright and intelligent

I just need adaptations
In this world not built for me
Patience and understanding
Kindness and empathy

Stable

I am a mountain
Steady in the raging storm
Of life which surrounds

Love

Love is an action
A commitment and feeling.
A constant devotion
True love is not fleeting

Love is a yearning
Trusting and true
Love is learning.
Accepting.
You.

Encompassing everything
Embracing flaws
Enriching lives
Love is not forced

Love knows no bounds
It goes on and on
Endless like a circle
True love journeys on

Through battles and triumphs
Love holds on
Standing by standing up standing with.
Love gives
Love is strong

Drifting

Drifting, floating, waiting
Waiting until I find a spot
Where I can rest until I'm lifted again
Through the air, through the breeze
Through the now

I'm falling gently
Rising sharply
Tossing
Folding
Flying.

Endlessly until I stop.

Buffered by the wind and by the air
Graciously until I coalesce
With my brothers and sisters who have
journeyed before me
On the winds, in the air, through the mists

When I stop
When I rest
When I sit
I no longer drift

I have settled
Before rising
Rising and journeying on the winds once more

Executive Function

It's really quite hard
To remember all the things
That need to be done

ASC

Anxious
Unique
Trusting
Insecure
Sensory
Tenacious
Insensitive
Caring

Overload

Shame.
Guilt.
Shutdown
I sob on the icy ground
My little girl
"What's wrong mummy? It's ok"

Intensifying with each word muttered by her
precious voice

The lights were piercing
The noises penetrating
Then the unkindness of the driver
It was all too much

Declined.
Sobbing can't think can't regain control.
Sinking back out into the stabbing cold,
The darkness of the sky comforting
Banging on the window.

Yet more input.

Explaining
More explanation
Exhaustion.

Then smiles.
And kindness.

From some

I sit in the warmth
My little girl sings
And still I sob

I cannot control

Emotions.
Overwhelming me.

Everything.
Overwhelming me.

I wish I could stop
It could stop.

I wish it could stop.

Eventually it stops.

Until the next time.

Spectrum

The spectrum isn't linear
Instead it's rather round
Different strengths and weaknesses
For each Autistic that I've found

That's why it's so frustrating
When I'm asked "just how severe?"
It's different strokes for different folks
Not a contest to find the "worst" one here

High functioning is just a buzzword
For those who have learned to mask
All our traits deemed 'inappropriate'
And who have stepped up to the task

A task that leaves us weary through our efforts
to fit in
Exhausted and drowning in this world we're
living in

Autism is not a spectrum
Don't make us toe your line
Instead see us on our beautiful wheel
Where with our differences we shine.

For my nan

It's hard to find the words,
It's hard to find a way.
It's hard to keep on smiling,
When we miss you everyday.

I thank you for your laughter,
I thank you for your fight.
I thank you for your spirit,
I thank you for your life.

And sometimes when it gets too much,
I stop and think of you.
I think of all the lives you've touched,
I think of you as you.

I remember you as Nanny Dot.
Sat in her dear chair.
Laughing, joking, smiling.
Living without a care.

You taught me how to live.
And what it feels to cry.
You showed me how to cope with life.
You showed me how to try.

And it comforts me to know, that God has you
by his side.
Because I know that you're still smiling,

That lovely little smile
X

The mask

I'm 33 years old now
And my mask is wearing thin
My mask that until just weeks ago
I didn't know I was living in

The mask of acceptability
Where I have learnt just how
To walk talk speak and function
To improvise
And now...

The mask is starting to crumble
I'm learning what's within
I'm starting to understand that it's not me who
should fit in

That I should not fix the 'problem'
When people cannot cope
With my traits and my 'dysfunctions'
Because you see I'm finding hope

That it's not my responsibility to hide just who I
am
For the comfort of others
Who just don't understand

That actually it's not my job to hide my
disability
Instead it's their job to understand
And extend some empathy

So yes my mask is slipping
And that journey I have found
Is really rather painful
When surrounding all around

Are people who don't get it
And worse yet just won't try
But it's ok
this is me
And My head?
It stays held high

Emotional skin

Feeling too much is
Both a blessing and a curse
When your skin is raw

Love language

My love language is complicated
It's not simple you see
My mask means I've gained knowledge of
what's expected of me

So I give lots of gifts and presents
And struggle to understand
That sometimes it's not wanted
Instead a different plan

Perhaps I'll work myself to death
In service of you
Barely coming up for air
Until my soul turns blue

Then you disrespect me
As by giving more and more
I'm easier to walk over
"You enjoy it" you implore

Me? I love hugs and affection
Ive been told I want too much
Deep consoling cuddles
But only from the one I love

Everyone to date
Has found me too intense
My love language too different
My emotions too immense

But I think it might be different
This time round you see
I think I may have finally found a friend
who accepts me for me.

Dysregulation

The buzzings setting in again.
The wave of numbness crashing in
Everything is foggy
Disconnected from my surroundings

What is real?
Am I real?
Why can't I feel?

Hot prickly heat all over my skin
I am not here
I am outside myself

Who am
What am
Where am
I

Spin

Special interests
Are nurturing for our souls
Crucial for our health

The distance

When my foot first hits the pavement
And I travel along the road
Which stretches out before me
My mind tries not to implode

This task is far too big for you
What have you to prove?
Why push yourself through gruelling miles
Why force yourself to move?

What benefit will this bring?
It's cold gruesome and wet
You'd be better off heading back
And giving up and yet...

Another voice within me
Begins to take a hold
It reminds me why I do this
When all is said and told

I don't do this for glory
For medals or for times
Instead I do this for the joy
For friendships that define

That define the soul of who I am
And why I choose to run
Why I choose to push myself
When it seems no fun

I do it for my health
And overall wellbeing
Without a run I flounder
With a run it's freeing

Freeing to push my body
And challenge all my limits
To see what strengths within me
To see what makes my spirit

For runnings not about
What you can or cannot do
It's about the choices that you make
And honouring you

Relentless forward progress
Is the mantra in my mind
This is why I go the distance.
It's why I won't get left behind.

Smile

You?! She said aghast and shocked her mouth
hung open wide.
But you are always smiling? You can't be sad
inside?

You see this smile I wear so widely?
It has so many fooled.
I paint it on each morning from my arsenal of
tools.
To look at me you'd never guess that anything is
wrong.
But the truth is that I'm drowning and I'm trying
to keep strong.

A creeping sense of sadness pervades inside my
bones. Its deafening in silence - when I am all
alone.
Sometimes I can't stop crying. Sometimes I
cannot move. It has no rhyme or reason, I know
there is nothing to prove.

A smile is so deceiving, it covers many things.
Like the fear sorrow and sadness that the big
black dog can bring.

But a smile is optimistic and filled with so much
hope. In truth it is my smile I use to teach me
how to cope.

The river

Dont mistake my tears for weakness
For instead they are my strength
My pain no longer resides inside of me

To release my tears is freeing
Even though I'm overwhelmed
When the sorrow overcomes me
And the river it flows and shows
Just how much I feel
How much I think
How much I am

When the river flows forth from within me
There is no stopping it's path
I will not drown or flounder in its waters
Instead I will swim
I will travel
Downstream to the sea
Where I float
Upon feelings upon emotions upon sadness
Present.
Now.